000106601

DISCARD

921
WIE
C. 1

*Bearing Witness*

# ELIE WIESEL

*by Michael Pariser*

*A Gateway Biography*
*The Millbrook Press*
*Brookfield, Connecticut*

*Dedicated to the memory of my mother's brother, Avorhom Abramowitz, whose last known act on earth was tossing two pieces of bread over a fence separating him from his sister and aunt at the Stutthof concentration camp in Poland. He was fourteen years old.*

Cover photograph courtesy of Bettmann
Background cover photograph courtesy of Superstock

Library of Congress Cataloging-in-Publication Data
Pariser, Michael, 1955–
Elie Wiesel : bearing witness / by Michael Pariser.
p. cm. — (A Gateway biography)
Includes bibliographical references and index.
Summary: Tells the life story of the Holocaust survivor who went on to become a writer and humanitarian and won the Nobel Peace Prize.
ISBN 1-56294-419-3 (lib. bdg.)   ISBN 1-56294-743-5 (pbk.)
1. Wiesel, Elie, 1928–   —Biography—Juvenile literature.
2. Authors, French—20th century—Biography—Juvenile literature.
3. Holocaust survivors—Biography—Juvenile literature. 4. Jewish authors—Biography—Juvenile literature. [. Wiesel, Elie, 1928–   .
2. Authors, French. 3. Holocaust, Jewish (1939–1945)]
I. Title. II. Series.
PQ2683.I32Z82   1992
813'.54—dc20   [B]   93-37126   CIP   AC

Photographs courtesy of Bridgeman/Art Resource, NY: p. 4; The Bettmann Archive: pp. 7 (top), 39; Wide World: pp. 7 (bottom), 41; Giraudon/Art Resource, NY: p. 9; YIVO Institute for Jewish Research: p. 12; United States Holocaust Memorial Museum: pp. 15 (top, courtesy of Norman Salsitz), 19, 33 (top, courtesy of D. Stevens), 42, 44; National Archives: pp. 15 (bottom), 33 (bottom, courtesy of the USHMM), 34; Yad Vashem, Jerusalem, Israel, courtesy of the USHMM: p. 21 (both); Government Press Office, Jerusalem, Israel, courtesy of the USHMM: p. 25 (top), Buchenwald Gedenkstaette, Buchenwald, Germany, courtesy of the USHMM: p. 25 (bottom); Laenderpress, Dusseldorf, Germany, courtesy of the USHMM: p. 28.

Published by The Millbrook Press
2 Old New Milford Road
Brookfield, Connecticut 06804

Copyright © 1994 by Michael Pariser
All rights reserved
Printed in the United States of America
5  4  3  2  1

*Elie Wiesel*

Mill brook

A *love of books and storytelling has long been a part of Judaism. Elie Wiesel felt this love early in his life. This painting shows Jewish learned men, or rabbis, reading the Bible.*

**W**hen *Elie Wiesel* was a young boy, he would listen for hours to his grandfather's stories about *Tzaddikim,* Jewish holy men who talked to God in Heaven and worked miracles on Earth. Elie loved those stories of wonder and happiness and hope.

Elie would grow up to be a storyteller like his grandfather. But Elie's stories would not inspire wonder or happiness or hope. Most of his stories would be about concentration camps, evil places where millions of Jews and other people were murdered during World War II by German soldiers.

At that time, Germany was led by the Nazi dictator Adolf Hitler. Hitler was an anti-Semite, a person who hates Jews. There have been many anti-Semites throughout history, but none as murderous as Hitler.

Hitler believed in what he called "racial purity," the insane idea that the German people — especially Germans with blond hair and blue eyes — were superior to everyone else. He believed that Germany's destiny was to rule the world. And he believed that the Jewish people were inferior and should be destroyed.

Between 1933 and 1945, Hitler waged two wars. One was a war in which he tried to take over all of Europe. In this war he was opposed by the Allies, a group of countries that included the United States, Great Britain, and the Soviet Union. The Allied armies defeated Hitler's armed forces and kept him from taking over Europe.

Hitler's other war was a war against the Jews. Hitler's aim in this war was to kill every last Jewish man, woman, and child in Europe. He came very close to succeeding. Before the war, there were approximately 8,860,000 Jews in Europe. By the time the war was over, the Germans, under Adolf Hitler, had killed six million of them. The German effort to kill all the Jews in Europe became known as the Holocaust.

When Elie Wiesel was fifteen years old, he and his family were taken from their home and transported to the Auschwitz concentration camp. Elie and his two older sisters survived, but his mother, father, and younger sister were killed.

Elie not only survived, he went on to become famous all over the world. In 1986 he won an award for his stories: the Nobel Peace Prize. Elie Wiesel

*Right: Adolf Hitler, history's most murderous anti-Semite. Below: German troops ride into Poland. As Hitler's army conquered European countries, his war against the Jews spread.*

won this prize because his stories helped people remember what happened to the Jews in concentration camps. And remembering the past is important if we want to make sure that the terrible things that happened during World War II don't happen again — to the Jews or to anybody else.

**E**lie Wiesel was born in the Transylvanian town of Sighet on September 30, 1928. At that time, Transylvania belonged to the eastern European country of Romania. Twelve years later it would become part of Hungary. Elie's two older sisters were named Hilda and Bea, and a younger sister was Tziporah. His parents, Shlomo and Sarah Wiesel, owned a grocery store.

Like all the town's Jewish children, Eliezer, as he was called as a boy, began attending school when he was three years old. First he learned the Hebrew alphabet. Then he quickly moved on to study the Bible and, finally, the Talmud, the basic text of Jewish law.

But unlike other children, Eliezer was not completely satisfied with studying the Talmud. He

*A page from the* Torah, *the first five books of the Bible in Hebrew. Elie was a dedicated student of the* Torah *and the* Talmud.

longed to learn something beyond the ordinary. At that time, there lived in Sighet a short, skinny man named Moshe. He had a scraggly yellow beard and worked as a "shamm'sh," a man who did all sorts of odd jobs. Nobody knew very much about him, and everybody just called him "Moshe the Shamm'sh."

One night, after the evening prayer service, Moshe and Eliezer began to talk. Eliezer told Moshe that he was not satisfied with his studies and that he longed for something more exciting. Moshe agreed to teach Eliezer some of the mysteries of Judaism. They began to meet in the synagogue late at night, after everyone else had gone home to bed. There, by the light of a few flickering candles, Moshe would tell Eliezer about the Messiah, who was going to come down from Heaven and bring all the Jews to the holy city of Jerusalem, where he would establish a kingdom of peace.

*M*eanwhile, World War II raged throughout Europe. In September 1939 the German army had invaded neighboring Poland. Since then, it had been marching through Europe, conquering country after country. In June 1941 it invaded the Soviet Union. By then, the organized attempt to destroy all the Jews of Europe was well under way. Thousands of Jews were being killed every day at execution sites, death camps, and slave-labor camps.

The Germans tried to keep the killings secret. The victims who were rounded up and taken away were never told what was happening. They didn't realize they were being taken to their deaths. And many people who witnessed these things simply turned their heads away and pretended not to see.

In Eliezer's town of Sighet, which was now part of Hungary, the Jewish community did not know that the Jews of Europe were being wiped out. They did not know that their lives were in danger.

But they slowly began to learn the truth.

In 1942, when Eliezer was thirteen years old, the Hungarian government made a rule that all Jews who could not prove their Hungarian citizenship would be expelled. Many could not comply. Hundreds of Jews were brought to Sighet where they were loaded onto a long, black train and taken away, leaving behind only a trail of thick, dirty smoke. Among those taken away was Moshe, along

*Like the women in this photo, Moshe and the other Jews were loaded onto a train and sent away to be killed.*

with his wife and children. At first, people were in an uproar about the deportation. But gradually they stopped thinking about those who had been taken away. Things slowly returned to normal — until Moshe returned.

Moshe described what had happened. He and the others had been taken to Poland, where the train was turned over to the Gestapo, the German secret police. The Gestapo took the Jews off the train, marched them into the woods, and forced them to dig a large pit. The Gestapo then shot every Jew. They threw infants up into the air and used them for target practice. Then the Germans threw the bodies into the grave the victims themselves had just dug.

Moshe was asked how he had escaped. He explained that he had been shot in the leg. The Gestapo, seeing him lying there, assumed he was dead. He lay motionless in the mass grave, waiting until the Germans had all left.

Moshe told his story over and over, forcing people to listen to him. The Jews of Sighet listened, but they refused to believe him. They said he had gone mad.

Many years later, when Eliezer grew up and began to write about his experiences, the first thing he wrote was that the Jews of Sighet were the victims of a "terrible illusion." They believed, Elie Wiesel was to write, that in each human being there is a little bit of God. Because of that, they refused to believe that any human being could possibly have committed the terrible crimes that Moshe had described. No, they said, Moshe must be mad. And, again, life in Sighet returned to normal.

**I**n *1944, however,* things again changed for the worse. The German army marched into the Hungarian capital of Budapest. In Budapest, as in every other place they captured, the Germans forced all Jews over the age of six to wear yellow stars on their clothes. Those stars were meant to humiliate the Jews and to make them easy targets for anti-Semites.

In Sighet the Germans created two ghettos, sections of town that were sealed off from the rest of the population. All the Jews were ordered to move into those overcrowded ghettos.

*Left: A boy around Elie's age at this time displays his yellow star. Below: Jews being ordered to move by German soldiers.*

**15**

Eliezer and his family did not have to move, because their house was within the borders of the larger ghetto. In fact, one of their windows looked out onto the rest of the town. They were forced to put boards over that window.

A month later, just as the Jews were beginning to adapt to ghetto life, word came that they were to be transported. Everyone asked the same question: Where were they going to be taken? There was no answer.

On the morning the Wiesels were taken away, Eliezer made sure he was the first one to leave the house. He didn't want to see his parents' faces. He knew if he did, it would make him cry. As he stood outside with all the other Jews, Eliezer caught sight of his seven-year-old sister, Tziporah. She was biting her lip to keep from crying. He knew that she was even more frightened than he was.

Eliezer and his family were taken to the smaller Sighet ghetto. After a few days they and the last remaining Jews of Sighet were marched through the main street of the village. Many of their non-Jewish neighbors watched from behind shuttered windows. Eliezer sensed that they were waiting for the last Jews to be gone so they could swoop down, ransack the Jewish homes, and steal whatever property remained.

They did not have long to wait. Sighet was soon *Judenrein,* the German word for "Jew-free" that, by the end of the war, would apply to thousands of once-thriving Jewish communities.

*he Jews were* taken to a train station, where two grinning Gestapo officers herded them into cattle cars, eighty people to a car. There were no seats, and there was very little room. They were on the train for days, and there was not enough room for everyone to sit down. People had to take turns standing up.

They had brought food with them, but there was no water. By the second day, their thirst became almost unbearable.

The train stopped just as it was approaching the Czechoslovakian border. The doors were opened, and a German officer announced: "You are now in the hands of the German army."

Those words destroyed whatever illusions the

Jews of Sighet still had. They had finally been handed over to their enemies.

"There are eighty of you to a car," said the German officer with a cruel smile. "If any one of you is missing, you will all be shot." With that, the cars were sealed shut again, and the train resumed its fateful journey.

Three days later, the train reached its destination: Auschwitz.

The Jews were met by SS guards armed with revolvers and machine guns. The SS was the section of the German state police in charge of running the concentration camps and killing Jews. One of the SS officers ordered: "Men to the left; women to the right."

Only much later did Eliezer realize what those few words meant: that he was seeing his mother for the last time. He had no chance to kiss her good-bye, to embrace her, to say a few last words. He could only watch as she and Eliezer's sisters were led away, his mother stroking his little sister Tzipo-rah's hair as they walked.

Eliezer turned to his father and held on to him for dear life, terrified of losing him, too.

*The gateway to Auschwitz. The words above the gate read: "Work Makes You Free."*

"Line up in rows of five!" came the next order. As the bewildered new prisoners struggled to obey, a warm voice from the dark called out to Eliezer:

"Boy, how old are you?"

"Fifteen," Eliezer answered.

"No!" commanded the voice. "You are eighteen! Listen to what I'm telling you!"

Then the man in the shadows, a Jewish prisoner himself, turned to Eliezer's father and asked him his age.

"Fifty years old," said Shlomo Wiesel.

"No! Not fifty! Forty! Do you understand? Eighteen and forty!" said the man, as he disappeared back into the shadows.

Then Eliezer and his father understood. It was dangerous to be too old or too young in Auschwitz. In Auschwitz, as in other camps throughout Europe, Jews who were deemed able to work were "selected" for slave labor. Those who weren't — the old, the sick, the very young — were "selected" for death in the gas chambers.

The man in charge of the selection that night was Dr. Joseph Mengele, a cruel man who conducted inhuman experiments on the prisoners. As

*Top: Like Elie's family, the Hungarian Jews in this picture have just stepped off the train at Auschwitz. Bottom: Men and women are separated, and the selection process begins.*

the new prisoners were marched past him, he would examine each one for a few seconds and then, with a wave of the baton he carried, send the new arrival either to the right or to the left. One side meant life, the other death. But which was which? The prisoners didn't know. Each had to wait until Dr. Mengele decided his fate.

Soon it was Eliezer's turn. Dr. Mengele looked at him.

"How old are you?"

"Eighteen."

"In good health?"

"Yes."

"What do you do for a living?"

Eliezer thought quickly. What could he say? He was a student in a religious school. But would Dr. Mengele have any interest in keeping students alive? Eliezer didn't think so.

"I am a farmer," he replied.

The interview was over; the selection made. Eliezer was sent to the left. His father soon joined him. Eliezer felt relief. No matter what happened, at least for now they were together.

His relief did not last long.

Not far ahead of them was a ditch. In it, something was burning. An enormous fire sent flames shooting into the sky. At first they couldn't see what was burning. But as they got closer, they saw a truck pull up and drop a load of something into the ditch.

Eliezer saw it with his own eyes, but he could not believe what he saw. Little children. Babies. Infants. Being thrown alive into the burning ditch. "How is it possible?" he thought to himself. "How can this be happening?" It was like some horrible nightmare.

"If only you could have gone with your mother," Eliezer's father said, his voice full of tears. Eliezer understood why his father was crying: He did not want to see his son die.

As they were marched closer and closer to the ditch, Eliezer decided that rather than let himself be thrown into the fire, he would try to break away and throw himself against the electrified fence that surrounded the camp. Death would be quicker and less painful that way. He got ready. They were only a few feet away. Eliezer could feel the terrible heat on his face. They were two steps away. Eliezer was about to run. At that moment, they were ordered to turn away.

They were safe. But for how long?

**E**liezer and his father were not kept at Auschwitz very long. Before they left, they had numbers tattooed on their arms. Eliezer's number was A-7713. From that moment on, every time he spoke to a guard or any other camp official, Eliezer had to identify himself as "Number A-7713."

Eliezer and his father were soon transported to the labor camp at Buna, an oil factory. Spared the gas chambers, they were now to be used as slave labor.

Being sent to a Nazi labor camp did not only mean having to work very hard. The prisoners in these camps were treated so badly that many of them died within a few months. They were subjected to torture and vicious beatings by the guards. They lived in filthy, horribly crowded conditions. They were terrorized by periodic "selections," during which the weakest workers were taken away and killed. And, more than anything

*Left: Two young prisoners of Auschwitz display their numbers. Below: The men in this photo are prisoners in hard labor at Buchenwald camp. Elie and his father were labor camp prisoners and also wound up at Buchenwald.*

else, they suffered from constant, unending hunger. The prisoners were fed only a cup of black coffee in the morning, and a bowl of thin, watery soup and a crust of bread at night. It was no wonder that while many prisoners died as a result of the torture and the beatings, many more died of starvation.

One bright Sunday morning, American planes bombed Buna. During the air raid, the prisoners had to remain in the barracks, exposed to the danger of falling bombs, while the SS guards headed for bomb shelters.

The barracks shook from the force of the explosions, but the prisoners were not afraid. They would gladly have given their lives to see Buna destroyed.

When the air raid was over, things went back to normal. But there was one difference: the fear and panic on the faces of the SS guards. Eliezer took this to mean that Germany was losing the war.

The summer passed, and soon it was time for Rosh Hashanah, the Jewish New Year, and Yom Kippur, the Day of Atonement. In normal times, observant Jews fast on Yom Kippur, a day on which they confess their sins to God and ask His forgiveness. But in Buna, as in all the concentration camps, the Jews were so close to starvation that to give up one piece of bread could easily result in death. Eliezer's father instructed him not to fast.

It was September 1944. Eliezer turned sixteen. And the first cold winds of autumn blew through the camp.

**W**ith *the arrival* of winter, life became even more difficult. Eliezer's right foot swelled up and became so painful he couldn't walk. He was told that his foot was infected, and that if he didn't have an operation right away, the infection would grow worse and his leg would have to be cut off.

Eliezer did not want to have the operation. Although he trusted the doctor, a prisoner who had been a famous surgeon, the hospital was nothing more than a barracks like all the others. And there were no drugs to put patients to sleep.

But the decision was not Eliezer's to make. The doctor had already decided to operate. The operation took an hour. Eliezer endured the first half

Life in the camps was miserable year-round but grew even worse during the winters. In addition to starvation, overwork, and gas chambers, prisoners were in danger from the cold. Here SS guards and their dogs patrol a camp on a winter's day.

hour of pain and then, mercifully, fainted. When he woke up, the doctor told him that the operation had been successful and that, with two weeks of rest, his foot would be completely healed.

Two days later, the Germans announced that Buna was being evacuated.

Twenty thousand prisoners left Buna on a brutally cold winter day, guarded by hundreds of armed SS guards. It was snowing heavily. The prisoners were ordered to run. Those who stopped for even a second were shot dead on the spot. The old and the weak fell in the snow and died of exhaustion and cold. Others were trampled by the terrified prisoners who were literally running for their lives.

The death march had begun.

Eliezer had not been able to find a shoe big enough to fit on his swollen, bleeding foot, so he simply wrapped it in rags. As he ran, the pain in his foot got so bad that it spread to his whole body. He grew weaker and weaker, but he forced himself to keep going.

After hours of running he was so tired that he was ready to give up, even if it meant being shot.

But he knew he had to survive. He was the only one keeping his father alive. So he closed his eyes and kept going. According to Elie, for a while he actually slept while running, until a push from behind woke him. He tried to slow down, but the crush of running prisoners wouldn't let him. The prisoners ran for over forty miles without stopping.

The entire trip took ten days. For the last part of the trip, the prisoners were crammed into open freight cars, packed so tightly they had to stand. They had no food; they had not eaten in days. They kept alive by eating snow. Since they did not have enough room to bend down, each man ate the snow off the shoulders of the man in front of him. The SS guards laughed at the sight.

Fewer than 6,000 men survived. Of the 120 men in Eliezer's freight car, only 12 were still alive when the train reached a new concentration camp: Buchenwald.

Soon after they arrived, Shlomo Wiesel became deathly ill. During his illness, an SS guard beat him for moaning too loudly. One morning Eliezer awoke to find that his father had been taken away during the night. He did not know exactly when his father had died, or even if he had still been alive when he was taken away.

Eliezer wanted to mourn for his father, but he couldn't. As hard as he tried, he could not cry.

After his father's death, Eliezer was sent to join the 600 children in children's Block 66, where he would spend his last three months in Buchenwald. By now he was so weak that all he could do was lie on his bunk. He no longer thought about his mother or father. Occasionally he would dream of food.

Meanwhile, the Germans knew the war was almost over. But their hatred of the Jews was so overwhelming that in the final days of the war they tried to kill every remaining Jew.

On April 6, 1945, the prisoners were told that they would no longer be fed. For five days, Eliezer had nothing to eat but grass and a few rotten potato peels he found in the garbage. During those same five days, the Germans began taking group after group of Jewish prisoners out of the camp and killing them.

Finally, on April 11, 1945, just as the SS were heading for the children's block, the American army arrived and liberated the Buchenwald concentration camps. Eliezer was free.

Three days later, he was hospitalized for food poisoning. For two weeks his condition grew worse and worse, until one day he happened to see his reflection in a mirror. He hadn't seen a mirror since before his family had left the ghetto, and he was not prepared for what he saw: the face of a skeleton. He was nothing but skin and bones. At that moment, two things happened: He smashed the mirror, and he became determined to survive.

Before he left the hospital, he wrote the outline of a book describing his experiences during the Holocaust.

**W**hen he was released from the hospital, Eliezer had no place to go. He had no home and no family. He was a war orphan.

A Jewish children's-aid group arranged for survivors of Buchenwald's children's block to be brought to France, where they were provided with a place to live and given a chance to regain their strength.

*Left: American soldiers lead newly freed prisoners out of Buchenwald. Bottom: The liberation of children's Block 66. The arrow points to Elie Wiesel.*

After the war, many of Nazi Germany's leaders were brought to justice in a series of trials at Nuremberg, Germany. Seated in the first two rows in this photo from the trials are eight of Germany's major leaders. Adolf Hitler and his two top aides killed themselves before they could be tried.

As a child Eliezer had often thought he might one day become a writer. But he knew he was not yet ready to tell about the things he had witnessed and experienced. He vowed to wait at least ten years before writing about them.

Meanwhile, he learned French. He enrolled in the Sorbonne University, where he studied literature, philosophy, and psychology. He was trying to understand how the things he had witnessed could have happened and to prepare himself for the day when he could begin telling the world about them. In 1948 he began working as a reporter.

One day in 1954, Elie was interviewing a famous Catholic writer, François Mauriac. Mauriac insisted on talking about the life of Jesus, his greatness, his divinity, his suffering on the cross. Upset with himself that the interview was not going as he had hoped, Elie blurted out that while Catholics love to talk about the agony of Christ, the Jews never talk about the one million Jewish children who had suffered so horribly at the hands of their Nazi murderers less than ten years earlier.

Then Elie grabbed his notebook and ran out of Mauriac's apartment.

Mauriac followed Elie out. With tears in his eyes, he asked Elie to return to the apartment. The older writer asked Elie personal questions about his experience, but Elie refused to answer, explaining that he had taken a vow of silence. Before Elie left, Mauriac told him that the time for silence was over.

Mauriac convinced Elie that the time had finally arrived to tell his stories. For the next twelve months, drawing on the outline he had written in the hospital ten years before, Elie wrote about everything that had happened to him from the time he was a thirteen-year-old boy in Sighet to the day the American troops liberated Buchenwald.

Elie called his book *And the World Was Silent.* Written in Yiddish, Elie's native language, the book was hundreds of pages long. It was published in Argentina. A shorter version, called *Night,* was published in France.

After *Night* was published, Elie took a job as a reporter in New York. That was what he did for a living. But the rest of the time, for hours every day, he would write his books. Having broken his ten-year silence, Elie now believed that it was his duty to bear witness, to testify, about what he had seen and heard and lived through.

Elie knew he could not make people understand places like Auschwitz and Buchenwald. Such evil could not be understood. But he could try to teach people what had happened by telling stories about the people who had died and about the people who had survived.

Elie's second book, *Dawn,* was a novel about a young concentration-camp survivor. In 1961, after writing *Dawn,* Elie was hit by a taxi while crossing the street in New York's Times Square. For many days, the doctors who operated on him didn't know whether he would live or die. But, once again, Elie survived. When he left the hospital, he wrote his third book, *The Accident,* about a concentration-camp survivor who is hurt in a traffic accident.

Not all of Elie's books were about the Holocaust. In the 1960s, when Jews were being oppressed and persecuted in the Soviet Union, Elie went to Moscow to witness the situation firsthand. When he returned, he wrote *The Jews of Silence.* That book became very influential in the movement that eventually helped millions of Soviet Jews immigrate to Israel and the United States.

In 1969, Elie Wiesel married Marion Erster Rose. Three years later, they had a son who they named Shlomo Elisha Wiesel. For Elie, having a child, and giving that child his father's name, were powerful symbols of Jewish survival.

Because of his experience at the hands of the Nazis, Elie was always sensitive to the sufferings of others. He believed that the Holocaust was a uniquely Jewish experience; yet it contained lessons that were universal. The hatred and racism that led to the concentration camps still exist, he argued, and therefore we must always be on our guard against them.

During the 1970s, Elie spoke out against the South African government's policy of apartheid. Apartheid not only forced the country's black citizens to live separately from whites, but it also denied them any say in running the country.

In 1980, Elie traveled to a remote town on the border between Thailand and Cambodia as part of an international effort to deliver food to starving Cambodians. When a journalist asked him why he

*South African blacks flee tear gas meant to break up their anti-apartheid protest. Elie Wiesel spoke out against apartheid and other injustices throughout the world.*

was there, he said it was because when he was starving in a Nazi concentration camp nobody came to help him.

Over the course of his career, Elie received many awards. He received his greatest award in 1986: the Nobel Peace Prize. The committee that gave him the award referred to him as "a messenger to mankind."

When he accepted the award, Elie spoke about the fact that the world knew what was happening in Auschwitz and the other concentration camps, but no one did anything about it. "And that is why I swore never to be silent whenever and wherever human beings endure suffering and humiliation," he said.

**E**lie Wiesel came a long way from that day in 1945 when American soldiers found him, starving and near death, in the Buchenwald concentration camp.

In 1993, almost half a century later, the acclaimed author, humanitarian, and Nobel laureate rose to address President Bill Clinton, Vice Presi-

*Elie Wiesel holds his Nobel Peace Prize medal and certificate. To his left are his son, Shlomo Elisha, and wife, Marion. At his right is the chairman of the Nobel Peace Prize Committee, Egil Aarvik.*

*Lighting an eternal flame at the United States Holocaust
Memorial Museum dedication. On the left is chairman
of the U.S. Holocaust Memorial Council Bud Meyerhoff,
with President Bill Clinton and Elie Wiesel.*

dent Al Gore, and members of the United States Congress at the dedication of the United States Holocaust Memorial Museum in Washington, D.C.

He spoke of the need to remember. "For the dead and the living, we must bear witness," he said. Those words, the words of Elie Wiesel, are carved in stone at the entrance to the museum.

He spoke of the difficulty of understanding.

"How can one understand that human beings could choose such inhumanity? How can one understand that in spite of everything there was goodness in those times, in individuals? There were good people even in occupied countries, and there was kindness and tenderness and love inside the camps among the victims."

And finally, he spoke of the lessons of history.

"What have we learned?" he asked. And he answered, "We have learned that we are all responsible, and indifference is a sin."

"We have learned," he said, "that when people suffer we cannot remain indifferent."

On that day, Elie Wiesel delivered a message of hope for all humanity: that men and women will never again be indifferent to the pain of others.

For the dead and the living we must bear witness

## Further Information

### Books to Read

### About Elie Wiesel

Green, Carol. *Elie Wiesel: Messenger from the Holocaust.* Chicago: Childrens Press, 1987.

### About the Holocaust

Abells, Chana B. *The Children We Remember.* New York: Greenwillow Press, 1985.

Altshuler, David A. *Hitler's War Against the Jews.* West Orange, NJ: Behrman House, 1978.

Finkelstein, Norman H. *Remember Not to Forget: A Memory of the Holocaust.* New York: Franklin Watts, 1993.

Stein, R. Conrad. *The Holocaust.* Chicago: Childrens Press, 1986.

### Place to Visit

United States Holocaust Memorial Museum
100 Raoul Wallenberg Place, SW
Washington, D.C. 20024-2150

# *Important Dates*

1928   September 30: Elie Weisel is born, in Sighet, Transylvania.

1942   First Jews are expelled from Hungary.

1944   Is taken to Auschwitz; stays with father but is separated from mother and sisters. He and father are transported to Buna.

1945   Death march to Buchenwald, where father dies. April 11: Liberation by U.S. Army.

1948   Begins work as journalist.

1960   Publishes *Night*.

1969   Marries Marion Erster Rose.

1972   Son, Shlomo Elisha, is born.

1986   Is awarded Nobel Peace Prize.

1993   Speaks at dedication of United States Holocaust Memorial Museum in Washington, D.C.

# Index

Page numbers in *italics* refer to illustrations.

Aarvik, Egil, *41*
*Accident, The* (Wiesel), 37
*And the World Was Silent* (Wiesel), 36
Apartheid, 38, *39*
Auschwitz concentration camp, 6, 18, *19*, 20–24, *21*, *25*, 37

Buchenwald concentration camp, *25*, 30–32, *33*, 37, 40
Budapest, Hungary, 14
Buna labor camp, 24, 26–27, 29

Cambodia, 38
Clinton, Bill, 40, *42*

*Dawn* (Wiesel), 37
Death march to Buchenwald, 29–30

Deportations, 11, *12*, 13, 17

Gestapo, 13
Ghettos, 14, 16
Gore, Al, 43

Hitler, Adolf, 5–6, *7*, 34
Holocaust, 6, 38
Hungary, 8, 11, 14

*Jews of Silence, The* (Wiesel), 37

Mauriac, François, 35–36
Mengele, Joseph, 20, 22
Meyerhoff, Bud, *42*
Moshe the Shamm'sh, 10, 11, 13–14

*Night* (Wiesel), 36
Nobel Peace Prize, 6, 8, 40, *41*
Nuremberg trials, *34*

Poland, *7*, 10

Romania, 8
Rosh Hashanah, 26

Sighet, Transylvania, 8, 10,
  11, 13, 14, 16–17, *17*
Slave labor, 20, 24, 26
South Africa, 38, *39*
Soviet Union, 11, 37, 38
SS, 18, 26, *28*, 29–31

Talmud, 8
*Torah*, *9*
Transylvania, 8
*Tzaddikim*, 5

United States Holocaust
  Memorial Museum,
  Washington, D.C., *42*,
  43

Wiesel, Bea, 6, 8, 18
Wiesel, Elie
  *The Accident* by, 37
  *And the World Was
    Silent* by, 36
  in Auschwitz, 6, 18, 20–24
  birth of, 8
  in Buchenwald, 30–32, 40

in Buna labor camp, 24,
  26–27, 29
*Dawn* by, 37
death march to
  Buchenwald, 29–30
at dedication of United
  States Holocaust
  Memorial Museum,
  *42*, 43
education of, 8, 10, 35
in France, 32, 35
*The Jews of Silence* by,
  37
as journalist, 35, 36
marriage of, 38
Nobel Peace Prize
  awarded to, 6, 8, 40,
  *41*
Wiesel, Hilda, 6, 8, 18
Wiesel, Marion Erster
  Rose, 38, *41*
Wiesel, Sarah, 6, 8, 18
Wiesel, Shlomo, 6, 8, 18,
  20, 22–24, 27, 30–31, 38
Wiesel, Shlomo Elisha, 38,
  *41*
Wiesel, Tziporah, 6, 8, 18

Yellow star, 14, *15*
Yom Kippur, 26–27